Peanut Butter R~

The Collection o~

Re~

Introduction

One of America's favorite foods is delicious and hearty peanut butter in cookies, breads, and snack bars, but they can become expensive when picking them up at convenience stores or snack bars. Making some of your own snacks can be very beneficial, tasty and cheaper than buying them off the shelf. Peanut butter is a delicious ingredient that provides nutrition, fills you up and tastes delicious.

Peanut butter provides a myriad of benefits, but many shy away from it because of the amount of fat. The fat contained in peanut butter mainly consists of unsaturated fat, which is actually quite good for you. The amount of unsaturated fat contained in peanut butter is comparable to that in olive oil, and we all know how healthy olive oil is. Peanut butter also hosts many other nutritious elements. One of the major components is fiber. Fiber plays a role in controlling blood sugar and cholesterol levels, as well as maintaining a healthy digestive system, and is found in abundance in peanut butter. Peanut butter also contains a large amount of proteins, as well as copper, iron, and vitamins E and B3. Because of the large amounts of proteins and fiber, a small amount of peanut butter keeps you full for a long period of time, and is used by many to stave off hunger pangs while trying to maintain a healthy diet.

Now that you know what a simple step like including peanut butter in your snacks can do for you, what are you waiting for? Dive in to this book and start enjoying healthier snacking, along with all the benefits found in peanut butter. No need to stop and purchase prepackaged cookies and bars, you will have a full stock right at home. I hope you enjoy these recipes, and have as much fun making them, as we do. Welcome to the world of America's favorite peanut butter snacks.

Table of Contents

Introduction..2

Cookies 6

   Peanut Butter and Banana Cookies.....................6

   Classic Peanut Butter Cookies.............................8

   Hershey Kiss Peanut Butter Cookies 9

Muffins and Cupcakes...10

   Peanut Butter Muffins with Chocolate Chips.....10

   Peanut Butter Cupcakes and Frosting...............12

   Peanut Butter and Apple Streusel Muffins 14

Bars 16

   Butterfinger Crunch Peanut Butter Bars 16

   PB & Chocolate Marshmallow Bars 18

   Peanut Butter Granola Bars 20

Cakes 21

   Peanut Butter Crumb Cake................................21

   Peanut Butter Cheesecake................................23

   Banana and Chocolate Chip Cake with Peanut butter Frosting 24

Bread...26

   Peanut Butter Bread Loaf 26

   Chunky Peanut Butter and Banana Bread 27

   Sweet Honey and Peanut Butter Bread.............29

   Peanut Butter Pumpkin Bread...........................30

Drinks and Other Treats...31

Peanut Butter Banana Breakfast Smoothie 31

Chocolate and Peanut Butter Smoothie 32

Peanut Butter Rice Krispy Treats 33

Peanut Butter Fudge Bites...34

Conclusion...36

Cookies

Peanut Butter and Banana Cookies

Nutritional Information: Calories 164, Fat 9 g.,
Carbohydrates 19 g., Protein 4 g.
Serves 36

Ingredients:
- 2 c. all-purpose flour, spooned and leveled
- 1/2 tsp. baking powder
- 1/2 tsp. fine salt
- 6 tbsp. (3/4 stick) unsalted butter
- 1 c. creamy peanut butter
- 1 c. granulated sugar
- 1/2 c. packed light brown sugar
- 2 large eggs
- 1 tsp. pure vanilla extract
- 2 large ripe banana, coarsely chopped
- 1 ½ c. dry roasted peanuts, coarsely chopped

Directions:
1. Pre heat the oven up to 350 "degrees F" and place the racks in the upper and lower third.
2. Then, line 2 baking sheets with parchment paper.
3. In a medium bowl, add and combine the flour, baking powder with salt; set it aside.
4. Next, in a separate bowl, add and beat the butter, creamy peanut butter, granulated sugar and brown sugar with an electric mixer on medium speed for about 2 to 3 minutes or until evenly combines.
5. Beat in the eggs and vanilla; reduce the speed to low and gradually add in the flour mixture; mix just until combined.
6. Fold in the bananas and 1 cup of the peanuts.

7. Place heaping tablespoonful's of the dough over the baking sheets about 2 inches apart and sprinkle with remaining 1/2 cup of peanuts.
8. Now, bake for about 15 to 18 minutes or until golden; keep rotating the sheets halfway through.
9. Remove & let them cool slightly on the baking sheets.
10. Finally, transfer them to wire racks to cool completely.
11. Serve immediately after cooled or store in an airtight container at room temperature for about 5 days.

Classic Peanut Butter Cookies
Nutritional Information: Calories 252, Fat 13.6 g.,
Carbohydrates 29.7 g., Protein 4.5 g.
Serves 24

Ingredients:
- 1 c. unsalted butter
- 1 c. crunchy peanut butter
- 1 c. white sugar
- 1 c. packed brown sugar
- 2 eggs
- 2½ c. all-purpose flour
- 1 tsp. baking powder
- 1/2 tsp. salt
- 1 ½ tsp. baking soda

Directions
1. In a bowl, add and combine the butter, peanut butter with sugars altogether. Then, stir in the eggs.
2. In a separate bowl, sift the flour, baking powder, baking soda, and salt altogether.
3. Next, stir it into the butter mixture and place in refrigerator for about 1 hour.
4. Remove and shape into about 1 inch balls.
5. Place them over the baking sheets and flat each ball with a fork to make a crisscross pattern.
6. Now, bake in a preheated oven at 375 "degrees F" for about 10 minutes or until cookies begin to brown.

Hershey Kiss Peanut Butter Cookies
Nutritional Information: Calories 115, Fat 6 g.,
Carbohydrates 14 g., Protein 2 g.
Serves 36

Ingredients:
1/2 c. granulated sugar
1/2 c. packed brown sugar
1/2 c. creamy peanut butter
1/2 c. butter or margarine, softened
1 egg
1½ c. all-purpose flour
3/4 tsp. baking soda
1/2 tsp. baking powder
White sugar
36 milk chocolates, unwrapped

Directions:
1. Pre heat the oven up to 375 "degrees F".
2. In a large bowl, beat 1/2 cup of granulated sugar, packed brown sugar, peanut butter, egg and butter until well combined.
3. Stir in the flour, baking soda and baking powder to form a smooth mixture.
4. Form balls about 1 inch around and roll them in the extra granulated sugar.
5. Place them onto ungreased cookie sheets about 2 inches apart.
6. Now, bake for about 8 to 10 minutes or until edges are golden brown lightly.
7. Remove and immediately press 1 milk chocolate candy in the center of each cookie.
8. Finally, remove from cookie sheets and let them cool on wire rack.

Muffins and Cupcakes

Peanut Butter Muffins with Chocolate Chips
Nutritional Information: Calories 300, Fat 13 g.,
Carbohydrates 43 g., Protein 6 g.
Serves 18

Ingredients:
- 1 c. all-purpose flour
- 1 c. whole-wheat flour
- 2 tsp. baking powder
- 1/2 tsp. salt
- 2/3 c. reduced-fat creamy peanut butter
- 2 tbsp. butter, softened
- 1 c. packed brown sugar
- 2 large eggs
- 3/4 c. milk
- 2 c. (12 oz) semi-sweet chocolate mini morsels

Directions:
1. Pre heat the oven up to 375 "degrees F" and grease or paper line 18 (2 ½ inch) muffin cups.
2. Then, in a small bowl; add and combine both flours with baking powder and salt.
3. Next, beat the butter, peanut butter and brown sugar in large mixer bowl until creamy.
4. Add in the eggs and milk; beat until smooth.
5. Add the flour mixture into peanut butter mixture and beat until just blended.
6. Stir in the mini morsels and spoon the batter into prepared cups about 3/4 full.
7. Now, bake for about 18 to 20 minutes or until toothpick inserted in the centers comes out clean.
8. Let them cool into the cups on wire racks for about 5 minutes.

9. Finally, remove to wire racks to cool them completely.
10. Serve immediately after cooling or store in airtight containers for later use.

Peanut Butter Cupcakes and Frosting
Nutritional Information: Calories 275, Fat 10 g.,
Carbohydrates 42 g., Protein 5 g.
Serves 18

Ingredients:
1/3 c. butter, room temperature
1/2 c. peanut butter
1 ¼ c. packed brown sugar
1 egg
1 tsp. pure vanilla extract
2 c. flour
1/2 tsp. salt
1/2 tsp. baking powder
1/2 tsp. baking soda
1/4 tsp. ground cinnamon
3/4 c. 2% milk
For Frosting
1/3 c. peanut butter
2 c. confectioners' sugar
2 tsp. honey
1 tsp. vanilla extract
3 - 4 tbsp. 2% milk

Directions
1. Pre-heat the oven up to 350 "degrees F" and grease or paper line the muffin cups.
2. In a large bowl, add and cream the butter, peanut butter with brown sugar until light and fluffy.
3. Then, beat in the egg and vanilla.
4. In another bowl, add and combine the dry ingredients.
5. Next, stir in the dry ingredients into the butter mixture.

6. Stir in the milk and beating well to form a smooth batter.
7. Now, fill the muffin cups two-thirds full with the batter and bake for about 18 to 22 minutes or until a toothpick inserted in the center comes out clean.
8. Cool them for about 10 minutes before removing from the pans and then, shift to wire racks to cool completely.
9. For frosting; in a small bowl, cream the peanut butter and sugar until light and fluffy.
10. Beat in the honey and vanilla.
11. Next, beat in enough milk to achieve a spreading consistency.
12. Frost the cupcakes & then serve.

Peanut Butter and Apple Streusel Muffins
Nutritional Information: Calories 340, Fat 12 g.,
Carbohydrates 52 g., Protein 8 g.
Serves 12

Ingredients:
2½ c. flour
1 tbsp. baking powder
1/2 tsp. ground cinnamon
1/4 tsp. salt
1 c. packed brown sugar, divided
2 eggs
1¼ c. milk
1/3 c. oil
2 apples, grated
1/2 c. peanut butter
1 c. large flake rolled oats

Directions:
1. Pre-heat the oven up to 350 "degrees F" and line 12 muffin cups with extra-large or giant paper liners.
2. In a large bowl, add and combine the flour, baking powder, ground cinnamon, salt and 1/2 cup of sugar; whisk until blended.
3. Then, in a medium bowl, whisk the eggs, milk and oil until blended
4. Stir in the apples and add it into the dry ingredients; blend just until combined.
5. Next, stir in the peanut butter, flake rolled oats and remaining sugar until crumbly.
6. Spoon half of the batter evenly into muffin cups, filling each liner half full; top each with 1 tablespoon streusel mixture.
7. Next layer the remaining batter and streusel mixture. Press each down with a spoon.

8. Bake about 20 minutes until a toothpick inserted in the center comes out clean.
9. Cool the pan for about 5 minutes and transfer to wire racks until completely cooled.

Bars

Butterfinger Crunch Peanut Butter Bars
Nutritional Information: Calories 200, Fat 9 g.,
Carbohydrates 30 g., Protein g.
Serves 24

Ingredients:
Non-stick cooking spray
4 c. miniature marshmallows
1/4 c. (1/2 stick) butter
1/4 tsp. salt
1¾ c. (11 ½ oz) milk chocolate morsels; divided
2 tbsp. creamy peanut butter
3 c. toasted rice cereal squares
37 pieces (about 1½ c) Butterfinger bites candy;
roughly chopped
2 c. small pretzel twists, broken into 1/2-inch
pieces

Directions:
1. Line a 13 x 9 inches baking pan with foil and also leave an overhang on two sides. Spray the foil with non-stick cooking spray.
2. Then, in a heavy saucepan; add and heat the marshmallows, butter with salt over medium-low heat for about 5 to 10 minutes or until smooth; stir frequently.
3. Remove the pan from heat. Stir in 1 cup of morsels and peanut butter until melted.
4. Next, stir in the cereal, chopped Butterfinger and pretzels twists.
5. Stir in the remaining 3/4 cup of morsels and spread the mixture into the baking pan; pressing down lightly with greased spatula.
6. Now, let it cool for about 2 hours or until set.

7. Lift from saucepan and remove the foil.
8. Finally, slice it into bars with serrated knife.

PB & Chocolate Marshmallow Bars
Nutritional Information: Calories 240, Fat 13 g.,
Carbohydrates 31 g., Protein 3 g.
Serves 36

Ingredients:
4 oz. unsweetened chocolate, chopped
3/4 c. butter
2 c. sugar
3 eggs
1 tsp. vanilla
1 cup flour
198 g. marshmallow crème
2 c. semi-sweet chocolate chips
1 c. smooth peanut butter
3 c. crisp rice cereal

Directions:
1. Pre-heat the oven up to 350 "degrees F" and line a 13x9 inches pan with foil, with ends extending over sides; grease it with cooking spray.
2. Microwave the chopped chocolate and butter in a large microwaveable bowl on high for about 2 minutes or until butter is melted.
3. Then, stir well until chocolate is completely melted and mixture is finely blended.
4. Stir in the sugar, eggs and vanilla; mix them well.
5. Next, stir in the flour and spread it onto the bottom of prepared pan.
6. Now, bake for about 30 to 35 minutes or until toothpick inserted in the middle comes out clean; cool it completely.
7. Spread the dessert with marshmallow crème.
8. Microwave the chocolate chips and peanut butter in a large microwaveable bowl on medium for

about 2 minutes or until melted completely; keep on stirring after each minute.

9. Add in the cereal and mix well.
10. Spread it over the marshmallow crème layer and refrigerate for about 2 hours.
11. Finally, with foil handles lift the dessert from the pan before cutting it into bars.

Peanut Butter Granola Bars
Nutritional Information: Calories 300, Fat 13 g.,
Carbohydrates 40 g., Protein 8 g.
Serves 12

Ingredients:
- 1 c. light smooth peanut butter
- 1/2 c. honey
- 1/4 c. oil
- 2 c. large flake rolled oats
- 1/2 c. each wheat germ, raisins & chopped dried apricots

Ingredients:
1. Pre-heat the oven up to 350 "degrees F".
2. In a large bowl, add and combine the peanut butter, honey with oil until well blended.
3. Then, stir in the oats and wheat germ, raisins & chopped dried apricots.
4. Next, press it onto the bottom of a 9-inch square pan.
5. Now, bake for about 25 minutes or until golden brown.
6. Remove & cool completely before serving.

Cakes

Peanut Butter Crumb Cake
Nutritional Information: Calories 430, Fat 20 g.,
Carbohydrates 56 g., Protein   g.
Serves 15

Ingredients:
    1 2/3 c. (11 oz.) peanut butter & milk chocolate
    morsels; divided
    1/2 c. semi-sweet chocolate morsels
    2 1/4 c. all-purpose flour
    1 tsp. baking soda
    1/2 tsp. salt
    1 ½ c. granulated sugar
    3/4 c. (1 ½ sticks) butter or margarine; softened
    1 tsp. vanilla extract
    3 large eggs
    1 c. water
    24 pieces Butterfinger bites candy; roughly
    chopped

Ingredients:
1. Pre-heat the oven up to 325 "degrees F" and grease a13 x 9 inches baking pan.
2. Microwave 1 cup of peanut butter, milk chocolate morsels and semi-sweet morsels in medium microwave-safe bowl on medium-high heat for about 1 minute.
3. Then, microwave for an additional 10 to 15 second, stir just until melted.
4. In a small bowl, combine the all-purpose flour, baking soda and salt.
5. Next, beat the sugar, butter or margarine and vanilla extract in a large mixer bowl until creamy.

6. Add in eggs one by one and beat well after each addition.
7. Stir in the melted morsels and gradually beat in the flour mixture alternately with water until smooth.
8. Now, spread it into prepared pan and bake for about 40 to 45 minutes or until toothpick inserted in the center comes out clean.
9. Sprinkle with remaining peanut butter and milk chocolate morsels immediately.
10. Let it sit for about 5 minutes or until morsels are shiny; spread it evenly.
11. Finally, sprinkle with Butterfinger pieces and cool completely in pan on wire rack.

Peanut Butter Cheesecake
Nutritional Information: Calories 500, Fat 35 g.,
Carbohydrates 43 g., Protein 8 g.
Serves 12

Ingredients:
1 ¼ c. baking crumbs
1/4 c. butter, melted
2 pkg. (250 g each) cream cheese; softened
1 c. smooth peanut butter
1 c. sugar
2 bars (100 g each) Swiss milk chocolate;
chopped & divided
1 ½ c. thawed whipped topping, divided

Directions:
1. Mix the crumbs and melted butter; press onto the bottom of a 9-inch spring form pan and refrigerate for about 10 minutes.
2. Then, beat the cream cheese, smooth peanut butter and sugar with mixer until well blended.
3. Add in 1 bar of chocolate and mix well.
4. Next, whisk in 1 cup of cool whip and spoon it over the crust.
5. Place it in refrigerator for about 3 hours.
6. Now, microwave remaining cool Whip with the chocolate in small microwaveable bowl on high for about 1 minute.
7. Remove and let it cool slightly. Pour it over the cheesecake.
8. Finally, refrigerate until firm and ready to serve.

Banana and Chocolate Chip Cake with Peanut butter Frosting

Nutritional Information: Calories 730, Fat 48 g., Carbohydrates 70 g., Protein 13 g.

Serves 16

Ingredients:

For the Cake
Non-stick vegetable oil spray
3 c. all-purpose flour
2 tsp. baking soda
2 tsp. kosher salt
1 ½ c. sugar
1 c. (2 sticks) unsalted butter
1/2 c. (packed) light brown sugar
3 large eggs
1 ½ tsp. vanilla extract
2 c. ripe bananas, mashed
1 c. sour cream
10 oz. mini chocolate chips

For the Frosting
2 c. creamy peanut butter
1 ½ c. powdered sugar
1 c. (2 sticks) unsalted butter
2 ½ tsp. vanilla extract
Chocolate chips, mini chocolate chips & chocolate kisses

Directions:

1. For making the cake; pre-heat the oven up to 350 "degrees F" and coat the cake pans with nonstick vegetable oil spray.
2. Then, line the pans base with parchment paper.
3. In a medium bowl, whisk the flour, baking soda and salt altogether.

4. In a large bowl, beat the sugar, butter and brown sugar by using an electric mixer for about 3 minutes or until light and fluffy.
5. Add in the eggs one by one and keep on beating after every addition.
6. Next, beat in the vanilla and stir in the dry ingredients; beat on medium-low speed just to blend.
7. Add in the bananas and sour cream; beat just to blend.
8. Now, fold in the mini chips and divide the batter evenly among cake pans; smooth tops.
9. Bake the cakes for about 35 minutes or until a toothpick inserted into the center comes out clean.
10. Transfer them to wire racks and let cool in pans for about 10 minutes.
11. Finally, invert the cakes onto wire racks; peel off the parchment and let them cool completely.
12. *For the frosting*; beat first 4 ingredients in a medium bowl by using an electric mixer for about 2 to 3 minutes or until light and fluffy.
13. Next, place 1 cake onto a platter and spread over about 1 ¼ cups of frosting.
14. Now, place the remaining cake on top; cover top and sides of cake with the remaining frosting.
15. Finally, garnish with chocolate chips and kisses.
16. Cover and chill completely and let it set at room temperature for about 60 minutes before serving.

Bread

Peanut Butter Bread Loaf
Nutritional Information: Calories 158, Fat 7 g.,
Carbohydrates 19 g., Protein 6 g.
Serves 16

Ingredients:
　　2 c. white flour
　　1/3 c. granulated sugar
　　2 tsp. baking powder
　　1 tsp. salt
　　1 large egg
　　1 c. milk
　　3/4 c. creamy peanut butter
　　Strawberry jelly, optional

Directions:
1. In a bowl, add and combine the flour, baking powder, salt and sugar.
2. Then, whisk the egg and blend the milk and peanut butter.
3. Next, pour it into a greased 8 x 4 inches loaf pan.
4. Now, bake at 350 "degrees F" for about 50 to 60 minutes or until a toothpick inserted in the center comes out clean.
5. Cool for 10 minutes in a loaf pan and then transfer to a wire rack.
6. Finally, serve with jelly (if desired).

Chunky Peanut Butter and Banana Bread
Nutritional Information: Calories 235, Fat 10 g.,
Carbohydrates 33 g., Protein 5 g.
Serves 24

Ingredients:
2½ c. all-purpose flour
1/2 c. granulated sugar
1/2 c. packed brown sugar
1 tbsp. baking powder
3/4 tsp. salt
1/4 tsp. ground cinnamon
2 (about 1 c) ripe large bananas, crushed
1 c. milk
3/4 c. chunky peanut butter
3 tbsp. cooking oil
1 tsp. vanilla
1 egg, slightly beaten
1 c. milk chocolate pieces
Peanuts, chopped (optional)
Miniature chocolate pieces (miniature)
For making peanut butter frosting
3 tbsp. peanut butter (chunky)
2 tbsp. butter
1 c. sifted powdered sugar
1 tsp. pure vanilla extract
1 tbsp. whole milk

Directions:
1. Preheat the oven to 350 degrees F.
2. Mix the dry ingredients together in a mixing bowl. (Except chocolate chips)
3. Then beat the wet ingredients together until smooth.
4. Add the wet mixture into the dry mixture; stir just until combined.

5. Then, stir in the chocolate pieces and divide it into 2 loaf pans (8 by 4 by 2 inch.) that are floured.
6. Now, bake in oven for about 55 minutes until toothpick inserted in the center comes out clean.
7. Cool in pans for about 10 minutes; then remove and cool on a wire rack.
8. Wrap and store overnight before serving.
9. For servings, frost with peanut butter frosting; top with finely chopped peanuts and miniature semisweet chocolate pieces (if desired); slice before serving.
10. You can also store foil-wrapped bread in freezer containers or plastic freezer bags for about 1 month and thaw overnight in refrigerator or for about 4 hours at room temperature before serving.
11. For making peanut butter frosting; in a small saucepan melt the chunky peanut butter and butter or margarine.
12. Remove from heat and stir in the sifted powdered sugar with vanilla.
13. Next, stir in the milk (as desired) to achieve spreading consistency.
14. This peanut butter frosting makes about 1/2 cup.

Sweet Honey and Peanut Butter Bread
Nutritional Information: Calories 163.5, Fat 7.6 g.,
Carbohydrates 20.4 g., Protein 6 g.
Serves 20

Ingredients:
2 c. whole-wheat flour
2 tsp. baking powder
2 tsp. cinnamon
1 tsp. salt
2 eggs
1 c. chunky peanut butter, unsalted
1 c. milk
1/2 c. honey
1 banana, chopped

Directions:
1. Pre-heat the oven up to 350 "degrees F".
2. In a bowl, add and combine the whole wheat-flour, baking powder, ground cinnamon with salt, altogether.
3. Then, in a separate bowl, beat the eggs; stir in the peanut butter, milk, and honey 4.   Pour in the flour mixture and mix until no clumps remain.
4. Next, add in the chopped banana and blend to distribute evenly.
5. Pour the batter into 3 small greased loaf pans.
6. Now, bake for about 40 to 45 minutes or until a toothpick inserted in the middle comes out clean.

Peanut Butter Pumpkin Bread
Nutritional Information: Calories 230, Fat 10 g.,
Carbohydrates 32 g., Protein 4 g.
Serves 32

Ingredients:
3 c. sugar
15 oz. solid pack pumpkin
4 eggs
1 c. vegetable oil
3/4 c. water
2/3 c. peanut butter
3½ c. all-purpose flour
2 tsp. baking soda
1 ½ tsp. salt
1 tsp. ground cinnamon
1 tsp. ground nutmeg

Directions:
1. Combine the cinnamon, nutmeg, salt, sugar flour and baking soda in a medium mixing bowl.
2. Then, in another bowl, add and combine the pumpkin, eggs, vegetable oil, water and peanut butter.
3. Stir the pumpkin mixture into dry ingredient mixture just until moistened.
4. Next, pour it into 2 greased 9 x 5 inches loaf pans.
5. Now, bake at 350 "degrees F" for about 60 to 70 minutes.
6. Cool for about 10 minutes in loaf pans and then transfer to wire racks.

Drinks and Other Treats

Peanut Butter Banana Breakfast Smoothie
Nutritional Information: Calories 279, Fat 3.7 g.,
Carbohydrates 45.6 g., Protein 16.9 g.
Serves 2

Ingredients:
- 1 medium banana
- 1 c. low fat 1% milk
- 1 serving strawberry Greek yogurt
- 2 scoops chocolate
- 16 g. peanut butter

Directions:
1. Add all the ingredients into a blender or a food processor.
2. Add in some ice (if required).
3. Then, blend altogether until smooth.

Chocolate and Peanut Butter Smoothie
Nutritional Information: Calories 330, Fat 13 g.,
Carbohydrates 44 g., Protein 15 g.
Serves 1

Ingredients:
1 c. fat-free chocolate milk or low-fat chocolate
soy milk
1 ripe banana
1 tbsp. peanut butter
4 - 6 ice cubes

Directions:
1. Add all the ingredients into a blender or a food processor.
2. Add in the ice.
3. Then, blend altogether until smooth.

Peanut Butter Rice Krispy Treats
Nutritional Information: Calories 156.6, Fat 8.8 g.,
Carbohydrates 18.3 g., Protein 3.9 g.
Serves 35

Ingredients:
- 6 c. rice "krispie" cereal
- 1 c. Karo syrup
- 2 c. peanut butter, separated
- 1 c. sugar
- 1 c. chocolate chips

Directions:
1. In a saucepan, add and combine 1 cup of peanut butter, karo syrup with sugar; bring to a boil.
2. Then, remove from the heat and pour in rice krispie cereal.
3. Mix them together and put into 9 x 13 inches pan.
4. Next, mix 1 cup of peanut butter and 1 cup of chocolate chips in a microwave safe pot.
5. Microwave for about 30 seconds or until melted at a time; keep mixing after each interval until melted.
6. Now, pour it over the rice krispie treats.
7. Finally, place into the refrigerator and let set for about 2 hours.
8. Remove & serve.

Peanut Butter Fudge Bites
Nutritional Information: Calories 111.2, Fat 7.2 g.,
Carbohydrates 10.3 g., Protein 2.3 g.
Serves 49

Ingredients:
- 1 ½ c. granulated sugar
- 3/4 c. butter
- 2/3 c. evaporated milk
- 1/4 tsp. salt
- 1 ½ c. peanut butter, creamy or chunky
- 1 tsp. pure vanilla extract
- 2 c. miniature marshmallows
- 1 2/3 oz. plain chocolate candy

Directions:
1. Firstly, line an 8" square baking pan with parchment paper. Fold its corners carefully and tape the sides, if needed.
2. In a heavy 2 quart saucepan, add the sugar, butter and milk.
3. Place on medium-high heat and bring the mixture to a full rolling boil; keep stirring.
4. Reduce the heat to medium-low, and keep on boiling for another 5 minutes; stir frequently.
5. Then, remove from heat and let it cool for about 2 minutes.
6. Stir in the peanut butter until melted and incorporated.
7. Next, add in the vanilla and marshmallows; stir until fully melted and incorporated.
8. Pour the mixture into parchment lined baking pan, shake or tilt for uniform thickness.
9. While mixture is still warm, press the plain chocolate candy into the top of the fudge.

10. Now, refrigerate for about 4 hours. Remove & carefully lift out the fudge by grabbing opposite sides of the parchment paper.
11. Slice even rows between plain chocolate candies.
12. Repeat the same process until done.

Conclusion

Thank you for your purchase of America's favorite peanut butter recipes. We hope you have thoroughly enjoyed all of the tasty treats found within this book. Whether you are a cookie lover, smoothie drinker, or snack bar person, this book has the recipes for you. The next step is continuing to make the recipes that you liked the best and sharing them with your friends and family. Now you understand why America loves peanut butter and finds as many places to use it as possible!

Printed in Great Britain
by Amazon.co.uk, Ltd.,
Marston Gate.